THE STATE
TRETYAKOV GALLERY

History and Collections

Published by decision of
the Academic Board of the State Tretyakov Gallery

Director-General Valentin Rodionov

A little more than one hundred years ago, on August 31 (by the old calendar), 1892, the well-known Moscow collector, merchant and industrialist Pavel Mikhailovich Tretyakov met with the Moscow City Duma and offered to donate his already renowned picture gallery. It included 1,287 paintings, 518 drawings and 9 sculptures by Russian artists of the eighteenth and nineteenth centuries, and also 75 paintings, 8 drawings and 5 statuettes by Western European masters which had belonged to Tretyakov's brother, Sergey Mikhailovich, former mayor and likewise a collector of artworks, who had died not long before. The Moscow City duma was delighted and grateful to accept the priceless gift. From that day began the history of the public museum — the State Tretyakov Gallery — which is generally recognised and beloved as no other museum of Russian art.

The year 1856 is accepted as the founding date of the Tretyakov Gallery. It was then that young Pavel Mikhailovich Tretyakov obtained his first works by contempo-

The Tretyakov family home on Lavrushinsky Lane, Moscow
Photograph, 1890s

rary artists, having set himself the goal of creating a collection which, in future, would grow into a museum of national art. At the time, there was no such museum in Russia. The overwhelming majority of paintings by Russian painters were scattered throughout various private collections, while the more famous and official canvases resided in the Imperial Hermitage or the Museum of the St. Petersburg Academy of Arts. Among private collections in Moscow and St. Petersburg in the 1840s and 1850s there were some which could have become muse-

ums of national art (those of P. Svinin, F. Pryanishnikov and others), but did not. Their life-span was short and they all disintegrated with the death or, more often, with the bankruptcy of their owners. Only Tretyakov succeeded in turning his private collection into a true museum of national and historical significance, a museum accessible to everyone. This amazing achievement proved possible largely due to Tretyakov's active and goal-oriented efforts, and also as a result of an unprecedented upsurge of national consciousness in the 1850s and 1860s.

Pavel Tretyakov was born in 1832 in Moscow. He was raised at home, and his education was not so much systematic as practical. But the future collector early on cultivated a passion for reading, especially Russian litera-

4

Pavel Tretyakov's family
From left to right seated: Tretyakov, his sons Vanya and Misha, his wife Vera Tretyakova, his daughter Maria, Tretyakov's cousin, Maria Tretyakova; standing: the daughters Alexandra, Vera, Liubov
Photograph, 1890s

ture, which at the time was on a steady "ascent" of world recognition. This proved to be the main "university" of the Tretyakov brothers, and it shaped their high moral and ethical ideals. Pavel Tretyakov was a business-like person, and his business was booming. But as a typical "man of the sixties," that is, a representative of that generation of Russians who had matured during the rise of democratic sentiment in the 1860s, he firmly believed that "a fortune made at the expense of 'society' (the people) must necessarily be returned to 'society' (the people)

in the form of some useful institutions." Although formulated only in 1893, this ideal had been on Tretyakov's mind at the very beginning of his activity as a collector. In 1860 he wrote in his first will: "I leave capital in the amount of one hundred and fifty thousand silver rubles for the establishment in Moscow of an art museum or public picture gallery... For me, truly and fervently loving painting, there can be no greater desire than to lay the foundation of a public repository for the fine arts, open to all, beneficial and pleasing to all... I would like to leave behind a national gallery, that is, one comprising paintings by Russian artists".

By the early 1860s, Tretyako's collection had swelled to several dozen paintings not only by contemporary artists, but also by those of the preceding decades.

5

Ilya Ostroukhov, Alexandra Botkina (Tretyakova) and Valentin Serov on the veranda of Ostroukhov's home on Trubnikovsky Lane, Moscow
Photograph, 1900s

The collector paid special attention to the then burgeoning movement of Russian realism. "I don't need the wealth of nature, nor exellent composition, not effective lighting, no miracles," he wrote in the late 1850s, "....just give me a murky puddle, but let there be truth in it, and poetry; poetry can be anywhere, that is the artist's job."

It was only natural that such aesthetic views brought Tretyakov in the late 1860s into contact with a large group of realist artists who later formed the Society for Circulating Art Exhibitions, the largest artistic association in the entire pre-revolutionary history of Russian art. Beginning with the first exhibit in 1871, Tretyakov became the main buyer of works by the Itinerants (as the Society members came to be called), and in this way rendered an invaluable service to the artists themselves and , for that matter, to Russian art as a whole. Later Ilya Repin, one of the foremost Itinerants, would say: "Pavel Tretyakov carried on his own shoulders, alone, the question of the existence of an entire Russian school of painting." But the support in this case was mutual. Sympathizing with Tretyakov's noble goals, the artists quite often refused to sell their paintings until Tretyakov had seen them and offered his opinion.

The scope of Tretyakov's collecting activity and the range of his interests were truly amazing. Each year he bought a few dozen, and sometimes hundreds of works at exhibitions and from the artists' studios without stopping, even in all of his prudence, at very large expenditures if his plans demanded it. Tretyakov bought paintings without paying attention to the roar of the critics and the displeasure of the censors, as was the case, for example, with Vasily Perov's *Religious Procession in a Village at Easter* or with *Ivan the Terrible and His Son Ivan* by Ilya Repin. He would buy a picture even if it did not fully correspond to his personal views, but was in accord with the spirit of the time, as was the case with Repin's *Religious Procession in the Kursk District* whose social message did not quite appeal to Tretyakov. He would buy even if very powerful and respected authorities, like

Leo Tolstoy, disapproved (as was the case with Victor Vasnetsov's religious painting). Tretyakov clearly realised that the museum he was creating should suit not so much his own personal (or anyone's, for that matter) tastes and sympathies, as reflect an objective picture of the development of Russian art. And in many ways he succeeded.

When choosing works, Tretyakov looked for typical features of an artistic movement or time as well as high artistic merits. Perhaps for this reason, Tretyakov more

than any other collector was able to avoid narrowness of taste and other subjective limitations. Each new decade brought to his gallery new names and trends. The tastes of the museum's creator developed and evolved along with art itself.

Art first, everything obtained by Tretyakov was hung on the walls of his home on Lavrushinsky Lane in the quiet Zamoskvorechye district. But already by the end of the 1860s there were so many pictures that it was no longer possible to house them all. In 1872 he decided that a special building for the gallery should be erected adjoining the house. In the spring of 1874 the paintings were moved to the new, two-storey building consisting of two large halls. However, the rapid growth of the collection soon required expansion through special construc-

7

In the rooms of the Tretyakov Gallery, (original display)
Photograph, 1890s

tions. By the end of the 1880s the gallery occupied more than twenty rooms. With the construction of a special building for the gallery, Tretyakov's collection was accorded the status of a true museum, privately owned but public in character; it was a museum free and open almost every day of the week for all-comers regardless of rank or calling. In 1892, as mentioned above, Tretyakov donated his museum to the city of Moscow. The Moscow City Duma, now the legal owner of the gallery, decided to appoint Pavel Tretyakov its Trustee for life. Tretyakov died on December 16(4), 1898. During the last six years of his life he, just as before, worked untiringly on maintaining and enriching the museum he had created. As before, he had the almost exclusive right to select works from exhibitions and artists' studios. He obtained new works both with funds allocated by the City Duma and with his own money, donating such purchases now to the P.M. and S.M. Tretyakov Moscow City Art Gallery. Beginning in 1893, under Tretyakov's direct sponsorship the museum began to publish a yearly catalog with a list of all of the pictures in the main collection as well as new acquisitions.

Following Tretyakov's death, a board appointed by the Duma began to administrate the gallery. Among its members were well-known Moscow artists and collectors such as Valentin Serov, Ilya Ostroukhov, Ivan Tsvetkov and Igor Grabar. Over the course of almost 15 years (from 1899 up until 1913) Tretyakov's daughter, Alexandra Pavlovna Botkina, was a permanent member of the Board. She later wrote a book of memoirs about her father and his founding of the famous gallery.

In 1899—1900 the now empty Tretyakov home on Lavrushinsky Lane to which the gallery was attached was reconstructed and fitted for the gallery's needs. In 1901—02 the entire complex was united by a new facade built according to the plans of the artist Victor Vasnetsov. This facade imparted to the gallery an original architectural aspect which to this day distinguishes it from other Moscow sights.

In the early twentieth century the Tretyakov Gallery

became one of the largest museums not only in Russia, but also in Europe. It was steadily enriched with works of both contemporary and older Russian art. From year to year the number of visitors increased, and in 1913 reached more than 250 thousand (by the end of the 1970s and the beginning of the 1980s it reached almost two million). Between 1913 and 1918 on the initiative of the artist and art historian Igor Grabar, at that time the Trustee (for all intents and purposes, director) of the Tretyakov Gallery, the exposition was reorganised. If before the new acquisitions were exhibited separately from the main collection of Pavel Tretyakov, now the hanging of all works was brought in line with a historico-chronological principle which is followed to this day.

A new period in the history of the Tretyakov Gallery began in the late 1910s and early 1920s. It was characterised first of all by the rapid growth of the collection. Following the nationalisation of private collections and centralisation of museum collections, the number of the gallery's exhibits increased more than fivefold in the first post-revolutionary decade. Several small Moscow museums such as the Tsvetkov Gallery, the Ostroukhov Museum of Icons and Paintings, and the Picture Gallery of the Rumyantsev Public Museum merged with the Tretyakov Gallery. At the same time, a group of Western European works from the collections of Sergey Tretyakov, Mikhail Morozov and other benefactors was transferred to other museums. Now these works are kept in the Pushkin Museum of Fine Arts, in part in the Hermitage Museum and in other Russian and foreign museums. All this served to reaffirm the gallery's status as a major museum of Russian art, reflecting its past and present, which was in tune with the original concept laid at its foundation by Pavel Tretyakov.

During the past half-century the Tretyakov Gallery has become not only an enormous, world famous museum, but a huge academic center occupied with conserving and restoring, studying and publicizing the museum's treasures. The gallery's academic associates actively participate in developing questions of the history and theory

9

of Russian art, arrange various exhibitions of old and new art both at home and abroad, give lectures, conduct tours, carry out restoration and expertise work, and introduce new forms of computerised museum information. The Tretyakov Gallery possesses one of the richest specialised libraries in Russia, containing more than 200 thousand books on art, as well as a unique photo and transparency collection and large restoration workshops equipped with modern technical facilities.

The rapid growth of the Tretyakov Gallery's collection in the 1930s posed the question of urgently increasing available space. New buildings were constructed, and already existing houses adjacent to the Tretyakov mansion were added to the complex. By the end of the 1930s the exhibition and working areas of the gallery had been increased almost twofold. But even this was insufficient for the rapidly growing and developing museum. A plan was created according to which all of the buildings neighbouring the Gallery would be destroyed and new construction would take place, stopping only at the Obvodny Canal embankment (architects A. Shchusev and L. Rudnev). Another plan envisaged the construction of a new building in a new location, after which the entire collection would be transferred to its new home (the building on the Crimea embankment, architects N. Sukayan et al., 1950s-60s). After much discussion it was decided that the Tretyakov Gallery's historical home on Lavrushkinsky Lane should be preserved. Reconstruction and expansion began in the 1980s (architect G. Astafiev). In 1985 the first new wing was built: a depository including spacious storerooms for various kinds of art, and restoration workshops. In 1989 the second new building, the so-called Engineer's Wing, was complete and now houses exhibition halls, lecture and conference halls, a children's studio as well as a computer and engineering service. The reconstruction of the main building began in 1986 and was completed in 1994. During these years the new concept of the gallery as a single museum existing on two main territories arose. In the original building on Lavrushinsky Lane are concentrated expositions and storerooms of old art, beginning with ancient times and ending with the pre-revolutionary period. In the new annex on the Crimea embankment the exhibition halls are allotted to twentieth century art. Separate exhibitions of both old and new art will be organised on both territories. Reconstruction of the gallery on Lavrushinsky Lane gave neighbouring architectural and historical monuments a new lease on life. These include the church of St. Nicholas-on-Tolmachi (16th-19th centuries), which received the status of museum chapel, and city structures from the eighteenth and nineteenth centuries on Lavrushinsky Lane, where additional museum exhibitions will also be located.

The Tretyakov Gallery collection now boasts more than 100 thousand works and is divided into several historical sections: old Russian art of the 11th to 17th centuries which includes icons, sculptures, minor and applied arts (about 5 thousand works); painting of the 18th and first half of the 19th centuries, second half of the l9th and turn of the 20th centuries (about 7 thousand works); Russian graphic art of the 18th to early 20th centuries, including drawings, watercolors, pastels and engravings (more than 30 thousand works); Russian sculpture (about 1,000 pieces); a collection of old frames, furniture, applied arts, and a huge section of post-revolutionary painting, sculpture and graphic arts located in the Crimea embankment annex.

———

The collection of old Russian art in the Tretyakov Gallery is one of the most unique in the world in terms of the quality and quantity of pieces preserved.

The groundwork for this collection was laid by Pavel Tretyakov, who owned 62 icons from the fifteenth to seventeenth centuries. After the death of its founder, the collection was put up on permanent display. However, for the majority of collectors and researchers in Tretyakov's time, the old icon presented an historical or archaelogical rather than artistic interest. Recognition of the artistic value of old Russian painting came only in the early twentieth century, and this provoked a true "boom" in icon-collecting. In a short time large first-class collections were formed by S. Ryabushinsky, A. Morozov, K. Soldatenkov, and others. Most of these found their way to the Tretyakov Gallery. In the late 1910s and early 1920s a Commission for the Uncovering of old Russian Painting worked in the country. Many of the oldest and most valuable works of old Russian art were placed under state protection, cleared of later layers of paint and, in effect, preserved for posterity in that period of revolutionary confusion. A large number of these ended up in the Tretyakov Gallery. The collection continues to be enriched today thanks to the acquisition of more valuable works from private individuals. Although one may believe that the extant examples of old Russian art have been discovered, some unexpected and lucky finds are made even now.

The most precious part of the collection of old Russian art is made up of icons from the eleventh to thirteenth centuries, the oldest, pre-Mongol period in the history of Russsian culture: *The Virgin of Vladimir, The Ustiug Annunciation, The Virgin Great Panagia (Orans), The Virgin of the Tolg, St. Demetrius of Thessalonica* and others. Some of them were brought to Rus from Byzan-

13

The Virgin of Vladimir. First third of the 12th century. Constantinople
Wood, tempera. 104 x 69 cm

tium (*The Virgin of Vladimir*), and researchers trace the origin of others to the development of purely Russian artistic schools in Kiev, Novgorod, Yaroslavl, and Suzdal. Although each icon shows features characteristic of one or another period or school, all are painted in keeping with the lofty traditions of Byzantine art of the eleventh and twelfth centuries which lie at the foundation of the artistic culture of the entire Christian world. It can be considered a miracle that these divinely inspired, but at the same time extremely fragile creations of human genius have survived through the tragic ups and downs of history to our day.

During the late thirteenth and early fourteenth centuries schools remarkable for their original idiom began to emerge in Novgorod, and then in Pskov. Reflecting the

14

St. Demetrius of Thessalonica. 1108—13. Kiev
Mosaic. 223 x 132.5 cm (with frame) 214.5 x 122 cm (exposed area)

tastes of the merchant-craftsman class which played a pri-
mary role in these distinctive city-republics, the Novgorod
and Pskov icon-painters managed to essentially
reinterpret the Kievan-Byzantine tradition. Their icons, as
a rule, are smaller in size since they were intended
mainly for home altars and parish churches. The paints
are predominantly bright and saturated with color, and
decorative combinations of vermilion and ochre-yellow
tones are frequently used. These icons have a tendency
to be narrative, to "tell a story" while treating traditional
religious subjects and images. Icons depicting episodes
from the saints' lives were also widespread.

Muscovy became the largest center of old Russian art
in the fifteenth and sixteenth centuries. Its golden age
was linked with the activity of such prominent painters

The Virgin Great Panagia (Orans). First third of the 13th century. Yaroslavl
Wood, tempera. 193.2 x 120.5 cm

as Theophanes the Greek (originally from Byzantium), Andrei Rublev, and Dionysius. Their names, which have since become legendary, were preserved by history. Without exaggeration, Andrei Rublev can be called the most renowned painter of old Russia. His name is mentioned often in the chronicles; his manner of icon-painting was highly esteemed and considered to be the best already in the fifteenth and sixteenth centuries.

16

Artist of the school of Theophanes the Greek
The Transfiguration. Beginning of the 15th century (1403?). Moscow
Wood, tempera. 184 x 134 cm

As any great artist, Andrei Rublev succeeded in not only achieving a high degree of perfection and spirituality in his art, but also in expressing the most important ideals of life contemporary to him. His famous *Trinity*, dedicated to the memory of the great champion of Russian unity, St. Sergius of Radonezh, is the embodied symbol of the ideals of spiritual unity, all-encompassing love and self-sacrifice.

17

Andrei Rublev (ca. 1370—1430)
The Trinity. 1420s
Wood, tempera. 142 x 114 cm

From the early eighteenth century, during Peter the Great's era, Russian art gradually loses its former almost exclusive religious orientation, and takes on a distinct secular character. The style of Russian painting changes dramatically. The medieval flatness and distortion of figures makes way for a striving to produce a three-dimensional image of the visible world, shown in precise proportional correspondence and in a concrete spatial environment. Painting technique also changes: paintings are now executed primarily in oil colors on canvas, while the main materials of old Russian icons were wood panels and egg tempera. It is amazing how quickly the Russian artists were able to master a completely new painting system and technique. Already in works by Ivan Nikitin, one of the first representatives of the new trend in Russian art, and a personal pensioner of Peter I abroad (i.e. supported by a grant for study and work abroad), there remain almost no traces of former artistic traditions. His followers went even further.

The greatest achievements of eighteenth-century Russian painting are connected with the portrait genre. This can be explained not only by the general tendencies for all of European art which signalled the golden age of the portrait in France and England in the eighteenth century, but also by the special attraction of this genre for Russian masters who were always keenly interested in the individuality and character of their contemporaries. The portrait painters Fyodor Rokotov, Dmitry Levitsky and Vladimir Borovikovsky consitute the glory of Russian eighteenth-century art. The customary stylistic categories of Baroque, Rococo and Classicism do not really apply to their paintings, although elements of these styles can be found in the work of each of these masters. Their portraits are pervaded by a general poetic mood, an admiration for the beauty of the human

19

Ivan Nikitin (1680s - not before 1742)
Portrait of Tsarevna Natalia Alekseevna. 1715—16
Oil on canvas. 102 x 71 cm

face and heartfelt emotions.

The first works of the Russian portrait painters of the eighteenth century appeared in the gallery under Pavel Tretyakov and his successors, but the collection as it exists today was formed basically during the post-revo-

Dmitry Levitsky (1735—1822)
Portrait of Natalia Ivanovna Melgunova. 1770s. Oil on canvas. 59.5 x 46 cm

Ivan Firsov (ca. 1733 — after 1785)
The Young Painter. Second half of the 1760s. Oil on canvas. 67 x 55 cm

lutionary years when aristocratic estates were destroyed
and inherited treasures flooded the art market. Although
it yields in quantity to the Russian Museum in St. Petersburg, the collection of eighteenth-century paintings in
the Tretyakov Gallery is one of the best of its kind in
terms of quality.

Vladimir Borovikovsky (1757—1825)
Portrait of Maria Ivanova Lopukhina. 1797
Oil on canvas. 72 x 53.5 cm

23

Anton Losenko (1737—1773)
Hector Taking Leave of Andromache. 1773
Oil on canvas. 155.8 x 211.5 cm

By the beginning of the nineteenth century the Russian artistic school had substantially gained in strength and had developed traditions all its own. As before, its best representatives paid much attention to the portrait genre. The first half of the nineteenth century produced a number of excellent portrait painters. In the works of Orest Kiprensky, Karl Bryullov, and Vasily Tropinin, the traditionally realistic approach to depicting man is combined with romantic overtones and exalted treatment of nature.

This same period saw the emergence and flourishing of a national landscape school. Stylistically it was rooted in Western European landscape painting, but such artists as Fyodor Alekseev, Sylvester Shchedrin and others derived inspiration from the native scenery, constantly leaning toward a typically Russian, lyrical interpretation of the landscape image.

Against the background of Russian art in the first half of the nineteenth century two first-rate figures can be distinguished: Karl Bryullov and Alexander Ivanov. Both graduates of the St. Petersburg Academy of Arts — and the best at that — they entered into the history of art as reformers of the academic system from which they emerged. The most famous creations of these artists are the grandiose compositions *The Last Day of Pompeii* by Karl Bryullov (1833, Russian Museum, St. Petersburg) and *The Appearance of Christ to the People* by Alexander Ivanov (1837—57, Tretyakov Gallery). Both artists strove to depict an historical event in a way that would enable them to pose and solve fundamental problems of human existence. Bryullov shared the romantic interest in historical catastrophes, which he interpreted as the main moving forces of the historical process. Ivanov, on the other hand, sought these moving forces in the moral foundations of each individual, and human society as

25

Orest Kiprensky (1782—1836)
Portrait of Alexander Pushkin. 1827
Oil on canvas. 63 x 54 cm

a whole. His *Appearance of Christ to the People* is an image not so much of the miracle of Christ's appearance as the miracle of the moral transformation of people on different social levels and degrees of spiritual development, from the slave with a rope around his neck who is barely conscious of his human calling, to the prophet John the Baptist, elevated to the heights of spirituality. This picture, on which Ivanov worked for more than twenty years, was the true achievement of this great artist, the meaning and justification of his entire, difficult

Vasily Tropinin (1776—1857)
Portrait of Arseny Tropinin, the Artist's Son. Ca. 1818
Oil on canvas. 40.4 x 32 cm

life. The painting came to the Tretyakov Gallery in 1925 after the Rumyantsev Museum in Moscow was reorganised.

During the first three decades of the nineteenth century a new trend was taking shape in Russian painting, and it showed an ever-growing leaning toward the depiction of events from contemporary life and to the creation of images of representatives of the "lower classes" — artisans and peasants. The pioneers of this trend were Alexey Venetsianov, the first in Russian art

Karl Bryullov (1799—1852)
Self-Portrait. 1848
Oil on cardboard. 64.1 x 54 cm

28

Alexander Ivanov (1806—1858)
The Appearance of Christ to the People
(The Appearance of the Messiah). 1837—57
Oil on canvas. 540 x 750 cm

to sing the poetry of peasant labor and daily life, and Vasily Tropinin, who produced a series of poetic, though somewhat sentimental images.

Their younger contemporary Pavel Fedotov introduced critical intonations into Russian realistic painting. A born genre painter, he superbly understood the specifics of this kind of painting. His paintings are always entertaining and sharp-witted in subject matter, extremely dramatic in composition, very lifelike in conveying

Pavel Fedotov (1815—1852)
The Aristocra's Breakfast. 1849—50
Oil on canvas. 51 x 42 cm

mimicry, gestures and poses of characters, and precise in depicting everyday details. Fedotov saw the goal and purpose of his work in correcting social morals and psychological "warps."

Ivan Aivazovsky (1817—1900)
The Stormy Sea. 1868
Oil on canvas. 54.2 x 65 cm

The next stage in the history of Russian art — the second half of the nineteenth century — is represented in the Tretyakov Gallery especially fully by the best examples, composing the nucleus of the collection. Created under Pavel Tretyakov, this section reflects the phenomenal breadth of his activity as a collector. Here can be found the names of all the remarkable masters of the time, and almost all of their more significant works. After Tretyakov, this section was enriched either by separate pictures not purchased by the collector himself (often due to chance or other reasons beyond his control), or by studies and sketches which did not interest him generally.

The second half of the nineteenth century in Russian art passed under the banner of realism, which paid particular attention to the social aspects of Russian life. Striving to "comply with the needs of the people," the progressive-minded artists saw these "needs" in abolishing the "darkness of medieval ignorance," in exposing the dark, ugly sides of Russian reality.

One of the chief exponents of Russian critical realism during its initial stage, the 1860s, was Vasily Perov. In his pictures Russian reality is shown with such sincere sympathy for the simple man that the artist can be compared to his great contemporaries, the poet Nikolay Nekrasov, the dramatist Alexander Ostrovsky, and the writer Fyodor Dostoevsky. In the words of Ivan Kramskoy, Perov's chief concern was the wrathful "condemnation of evil." This was reflected both in his choice of subjects and in the way he interpreted them — the laconic drawing and restrained color scheme almost always give his paintings a sorrowful ring.

The highest achievements of Russian painting in the 1870s are connected with the activity of artists who belonged to the Society for Circulating Art Exhibitions. The founding of this society was an event of great histori-

33

Alexey Savrasov (1830—1897)
The Rooks Have Come. 1871
Oil on canvas. 62 x 48.5 cm

cal significance for Russian art as it ushered in a new era in Russia's artistic development. It was an era of rigorous democratisation in art, its emancipation from the control exercised by the autocratic and bureaucratic state through the Imperial Academy of Arts. The society's main goal, as recorded in its Charter, was to "cultivate love for art among the people". The Itinerants significantly increased interest in Russian art by reaching out to people in the provinces, and in this way earned nationwide respect.

One of the founders of the society, its idealogical leader and moving spirit, was the prominent Russian portrait painter Ivan Kramskoy. He, like most of the Itinerants, considered that the portrait must characterise a person first of all from the point of view of moral convictions.

Lofty ethical problems and meditations on the correlation between the personal and the public in human life became the subject of his *Christ in the Wilderness*, which is not so much a historical or religious work as a moral and philosophical one.

34

Vasily Perov (1834—1882)
The Last Inn at the City Gates. 1868
Oil on canvas. 51.1 x 65.8 cm

The realistic principles of the Itinerants penetrated all the other genres of Russian art, but first and foremost they led to the unprecedented rise of the everyday picture which most directly solved the problem of bringing life close to art.

Landscape painting developed very intensively during the second half of the nineteenth century. It can be said that the landscape was the true passion of artists of the time, especially of such well-known painters as Alexey

35

Ivan Kramskoy (1837—1887)
Portrait of Mikhail Saltykov-Shchedrin. 1879
Oil on canvas. 88 x 68 cm

Ivan Shishkin (1832—1898)
Rye. 1878
Oil on canvas. 107 x 187 cm

Savrasov, Fyodor Vasilev, Ivan Shishkin, Vasily Polenov, Arkhip Kuindzhi, Isaac Levitan and others. In their portrayal of Russian nature these artists pondered the life of the people, an approach characteristic for all of Russian culture.

The powerful development of democratic and realistic tendencies in Russian painting of the 1860s and 70s paved the way for the blossoming of the Itinerants' art in the 1880s. In the work of the greatest masters of the time, Ilya Repin and Vasily Surikov, the Itinerants' realism achieved the long-desired harmony of "truth" and "beauty."

Ilya Repin, a painter possessing an enormous gift, was, perhaps, the most talented of the Itinerants. Keenly sensitive to the life around him, he created his best works on the themes of contemporary Russian reality, among these such truly social epics as *The Volga Boatmen and Religious Procession in the Kursk Guberniya*. A number of Repin's genre pieces are dedicated to the

Fyodor Vasilev (1850—1873)
Abandoned Mill 1871—73
Paper, watercolor, gouache, whiting, brush, pen, scratching. 44.1 x 51.9 cm

populist intelligentsia *(They Did Not Expect Him)*, to their revolutionary struggle, with which the artist sincerely sympathised. Repin painted a few large historical compositions in which he sought either to reveal the dramatic aspects of history *(Ivan the Terrible and his Son Ivan)* or to show the Russians' love for freedom as a basic national trait *(The Zaporozhye Cossacks Writing a Mocking Letter to the Turkish Sultan)*. But quite possibly, Repin's favorite genre was the portrait. It was in portraiture that the distinctive features of Repin's gift made themselves most clearly evident: an irrepressible love and avid curiosity for life, interest and attention to man, an almost Tolstoyan ability to sense the uniqueness of the inner world of each individual, and ability to find ever new artistic devices for revealing this world.

Unlike Repin, an artist inexorably linked with contemporary reality, Vasily Surikov was first and foremost a "historian," the greatest of all Russian historical painters who possessed the gift of presenting events of ages long

Vasily Polenov (1844—1927)
Moscow Courtyard. 1878
Oil on canvas. 64.5 x 80.1 cm

Ilya Repin (1844—1930)
Religious Procession in the Kursk Guberniya. 1880—83
Oil on canvas. 175 x 280 cm

past as if he himself were a witness and participant. Surikov relied not on "archaeology," but on his own powerful artistic imagination, his acute and spontaneous sense of the past. He was especially interested in the turning points of Russian history. His best canvases are devoted to events of the seventeenth century — a time of numerous revolts and broad popular movements. Surikov

Victor Vasnetsov (1848—1926)
Alyonushka. 1881
Oil on canvas. 173 x 121 cm

loved brilliant and strong characters, but viewed history not through the eyes of an individual, no matter how significant, but through the eyes of the people, always the main and true hero of his paintings.

Arkhip Kuindzhi (1842?—1910)
After the Rain. 1879. Oil on canvas. 102 x 159 cm

Isaac Levitan (1860—1900)
Secluded Monastery. 1890. Oil on canva. 87.5 x 108 cm

Among the masters of Russian painting of the last three decades of the nineteenth century, along with Repin and Surikov, the names of Victor Vasnetsov and Nikolay Gay should also be noted.

Victor Vasnetsov made his artistic debut in the late 1870s and early 1880s. His pictures raised interest in Russian folklore by creating images from folk tales and heroic legends *(Alyonushka, Bogatyrs)*. Historic events and characters appear in Vasnetsov's works as they were preserved in the memory of the people. Vasnetsov's artistic quest coincided by and large with the aspirations of young Moscow artists who sought to revive folk forms in art and revitalise the Russian folk crafts (the Abramtsevo Art Circle).

Nikolay Gay entered into the history of Russian art as one of the founders of the Itinerants' historical painting. His approach to depicting historical events was strictly realistic *(Peter I Interrogating Tsarveich Alexey Petrovich in Peterhof)*. In the 1880s, greatly impressed by Leo Tolstoy' s moral and philosophical teachings, Gay de-

Nikolay Gay (1831—1889)
Peter I Interrogating His Son Alexey Petrovich in Peterhof. 1871
Oil on canvas. 135.7 x 173 cm

cided to create his own "Gospel in paints" as had his friend and teacher in writing. In his pictures on gospel themes the artist strove above all to show the collision of good and evil in human life and history.

The work of Vasily Vereshchagin, a painter of battle scenes, has a special niche in the history of Russian art of the second half of the nineteenth century. He was, perhaps, the only great master not belonging to the Society for Circulating Art Exhibitions but, just as they, he was moved by a general interest in the life of the masses. He saw his task in revealing the truth of war to his viewers "by means of paint," to show them what a "disgusting, dismal and colossal evil" the battlefield was. He depicted war as a display of barbarism, as a threat to civilisation *(The Doors of Tamerlane's Mausoleum)*.

45

Vasily Vereshchagin (1842—1902)
The Gates of the Palace of Timur (Tamerlane). 1871
Oil on canvas. 213 x 168 cm

Vasily Surikov (1848—1916)
The Morning of the Execution of the Streltsy. 1881
Oil on canvas. 218 x 379 cm

In the late 1880s and early 1850s a large group of talented young painters emerged on the Russian art scene. These included Abram Arkhipov, Mikhail Vrubel, Konstantin Korovin, Sergey Korovin, Mikhail Nesterov, Andrey Ryabushkin, and Valentin Serov. All or nearly all of them were pupils of their senior masters, the Itinerants, and seemed to be the direct successors of their realistic tendencies. But at the same time, the aesthetic aspects of their work began to prevail over social tasks that had so profoundly inspired Russian artists of the previous generation. The most important of this group of artists were Konstantin Korovin, Valentin Serov, and Mikhail Vrubel. They are known as untiring "seekers" of "untrodden" paths in art.

Korovin's artistic development was marked by greater simplicity and clarity than that of the others. From the very beginning he was drawn — in many ways spontaneously — to Impressionism. Later, the Impressionistic system came to underlie Korovin's entire creative method, bringing him recognition as the best Russian Impressionist.

Like Korovin, Valentin Serov began with devices close to Impressionism. His famous *Girl with Peaches* and *Girl in Sunlight* reflected the original aspirations of the young artist who sought the meaning and poetry of life in a harmonious fusion of man and nature, who wanted to express the feeling of "joie de vivre." Serov's further successes were connected with portrait painting, on which he left his mark. The portrait genre gave Serov the opportunity to implement different and sometimes quite novel ideas and stylistic experiments which distinguished his short but intense artistic career.

Perhaps the most original Russian master at the turn of the century was Mikhail Vrubel. Like the majority of the European Symbolists of the late nineteenth century,

---

Valentin Serov (1865—1911)
Girl with Peaches. 1887
Oil on canvas. 91 x 85 cm

Mikhail Nesterov (1862—1942)
The Vision of the Youth Bartholomew. 1889—90
Oil on canvas. 160 x 211 cm

he expressed his Symbolist ideas in stylistic forms which in Russian came to be called "modern," and represented a Russian version of the European Sezession. Vrubel often treated fantastic themes in his art: he was fascinated by the proud spirit of the evil Demon, the mysterious wood sprite Pan, and other mythical figures. Embodied in purely concrete forms, Vrubel's images, no matter how fantastic they might be, never left the realm of the real, and expressed the artist's romantic dream of the Beautiful and the Exalted.

Radical changes began to occur in Russian art in the early twentieth century. A crisis hit the Itinerant movement, and along with it a crisis of Russian classical realism as a whole. Russian social life changed drastically too. The former social ideals which had fed art exhausted themselves. The exposing, analytic approach to reality was no longer adequate to handle new problems. In the rapid and awesome development of life the task of art was not only to analyze, but to foretell the future. The structure of Russian artistic life became more complex and lost its former unity. If before, over the course

Alexander Benois (1870—1960)
The King Promenading. 1906
Paper on cardboard, gouache, watercolor, bronze and
silver powder, graphite, pen, brush. 48 x 62 cm

of two and a half decades, the Society for Circulating Art Exhibitions not only preseved its vitality, but also its attraction for each new generation, then beginning with the late 1890s various new artistic groups appeared, either coexisting with or directly opposing one another. The closer we come to the 1910s, the more dynamic and diverse the picture of Russian artistic life becomes. Thus began the era of individualism in Russian art. If in the

Victor Borisov-Musatov (1870—1905)
Lady in Blue. 1902
Paper on canvas, watercolor, pastel. 81.5 x 62.5 cm

Mikhail Vrubel (1856—1910)
Demon Seated. 1890
Oil on canvas. 114 x 211 cm

second half of the nineteenth century each artist revealed his individuality "within" one common method, without challenging it in principle, now each group of artists emerged not only with its own ideological slogan, but united quite different and sometimes diametrically opposed individualities, methods and stylistic devices.

The art of this period is represented fairly fully in the Tretyakov Gallery. Here one can find the most characteristic paintings and graphic works by a very influential group of artists that had united around the World of Art magazine: Alexander Benois, Konstantin Somov, Mstislav Dobuzhinsky, Evgeny Lanceray, Zinaida Serebryakova, Igor Grabar, Nikolay Roerich and others, with their refined stylistics and retrospective interest in European and Russian culture of the eighteenth century. There was the Blue Rose group and a related association, The Golden Fleece, which included Pavel Kuznetsov, Martiros Saryan, Nikolay Krylov, Kuzma Petrov-Vodkin

---

Konstantin Korovin (1861—1939)
Paris. Boulevard des Capuccines. 1911
Oil on canvas. 65 x 80.7 cm

and others who preached, at least in their early works, principles of poetic Symbolism introduced in Russian art by Victor Borisov-Musatov. The art of the young Russian avant-garde of the 1910s is also well represented at the Tretyakov Gallery, especially the most popular Jack of Diamonds group — Pyotr Konchalovsky, Ilya Mashkov, Aristarkh Lentulov, Robert Falk, Alexander Kuprin — as well as artists who had initially participated, then gone their own way: Mikhail Larionov, Natalia Goncharova, Marc Chagall, Vasily Kandinsky and Kasimir Malevich. The aesthetic program of this circle contained elements of quite different Post-Impressionist trends from Cezannism to analytical Cubism, decorative primitivism and other experiments in non-objective art.

The formation of the section of early twentieth-century art at the Tretyakov Gallery began in the pre-revolutionary period. Continuing Tretyakov's precepts, the gallery's leaders (Ostroukhov, Serov, Botkina, and then Gra-

Pavel Kuznetsov (1878—1968)
Sleeping Girl in a T ent. 1911
Oil on canvas. 66 x 71 cm

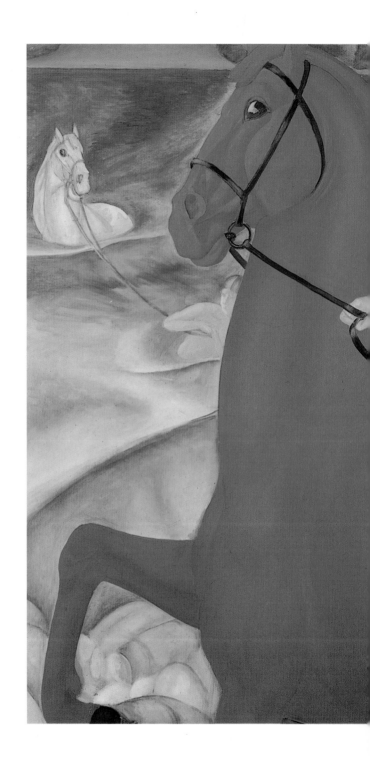

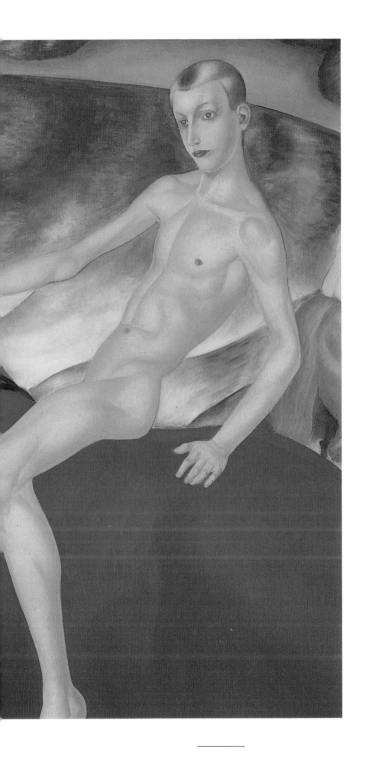

59

Kuzma Petrov-Vodkin (1878—1939)
Bathing the Red Horse. 1912
Oil on canvas. 160 x 186 cm

bar) carefully followed the course of development in Russian art, acquiring the first works of the young modernists Petrov-Vodkin, Kuznetsov, Larionov, Goncharova, Konchalovsky, Mashkov, Saryan and others. But the overwhelming majority of their works and those by even younger representatives of the Russian avant-garde — Kandinsky, Malevich, Chagall and others — entered the Tretyakov Gallery only after 1918 from the State Mu-

Natalia Goncharova (1881—1962)
Winter. Gathering Brushwood. 1911
Oil on canvas. 132.3 x 103.4 cm

seum Fund, from exhibitions, studios and private collections. The largest donation of avant-garde art was made
by George Kostakis in 1977.

Kasimir Malevich (1878—1935)
Haymaking. 1909
Oil on canvas. 75.7 x 65.6 cm

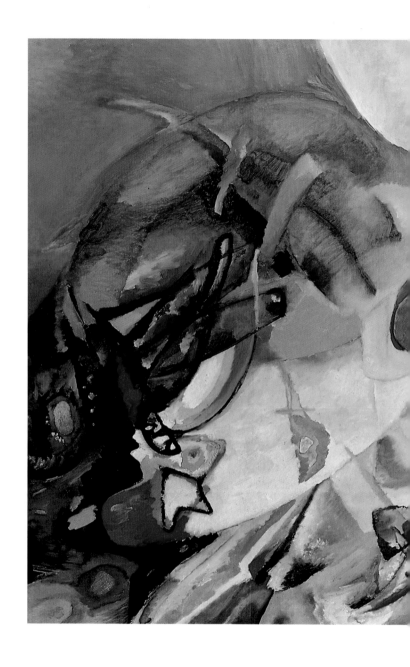